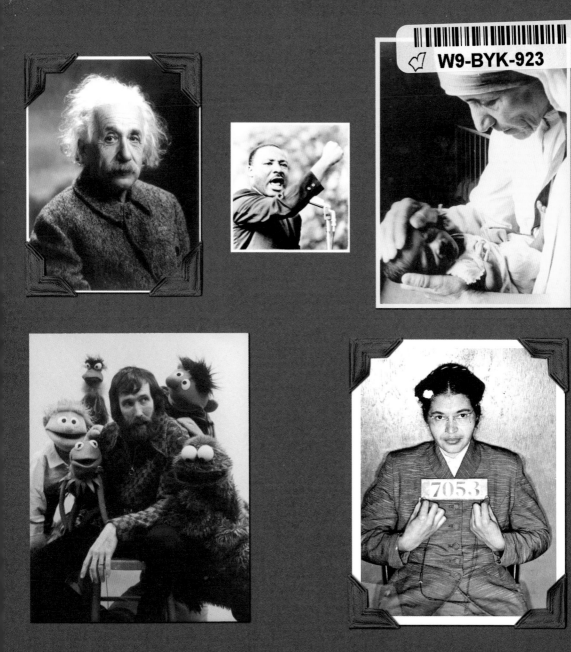

to: _____

a gift from: _____

heroes for
my son

heroes for

my son

brad meltzer

HARPER

An Imprint of HarperCollinsPublishers

www.harpercollins.com

FIRST EDITION

Library of Congress Cataloging-in-Publication Data

Meltzer, Brad.
  Heroes for my son / by Brad Meltzer.—1st ed.
    p. cm.
  ISBN 978-0-06-190528-5
  1. Conduct of life—Juvenile literature. 2. Heroes—Biography—Juvenile literature. I. Title.
  BJ1547.4.M45 2010
  920.02—dc22
  [B]
                                                                              2009051550

  14 CG/QG 10 9 8 7 6 5

For Theo and Jonas,

MY SONS,
MY HEROES

contents

Acknowledgments | x

Introduction | xii

The Wright Brothers | 2

Team Hoyt | 4

Joe Shuster and
Jerry Siegel | 6

Mr. Rogers | 8

Miep Gies | 10

Roberto Clemente | 12

Amelia Earhart | 14

Nelson Mandela | 16

Norman Borlaug | 18

Martin Luther King Jr. | 20

Anne Sullivan | 22

John Lennon | 24

Harriet Tubman | 26

Harry Houdini | 28

Jackie Robinson | 30

Albert Einstein | 32

Jesse Owens | 34

Jim Henson | 36

Jonas Salk | 38

Dr. Seuss | 40

Bella Abzug | 42

Dan West | 44

Mother Teresa | 46

Steven Spielberg | 48

George H. W. Bush | 50

Lucille Ball | 52

George Washington | 54

Charlie Chaplin | 56

Oprah Winfrey | 58

Officer Frank Shankwitz
| 60

Mark Twain | 62

Eleanor Roosevelt | 64

Neil Armstrong | 66

Paul Newman | 68

Pelé | 70

Barbara Johns | 72

Aung San Suu Kyi | 74

Eli Segal | 76

Abraham Lincoln | 78

Andy Miyares | 80

Clara Hale | 82

Muhammad Ali | 84

Barack Obama | 86

Harper Lee | 88

Thomas Jefferson | 90

Mahatma Gandhi | 92

Frederick Douglass | 94

Chesley B. Sullenberger III
| 96

Rosa Parks | 98

Lou Gehrig | 100

Teri Meltzer | 102

Ben Rubin | 104

Who Is Your Hero? | 106

acknowledgments

There are many heroes in my life. But my favorite ones are my little ones—my children—Jonas, Lila, and Theo, who are the three reasons this book exists. They teach me every day; they inspire me every day—and they are my truest dreams. My other hero is my wife, Cori, who gave me my greatest gifts and was the very first to believe. Thank you to my dad, who fed my love of heroes by buying me all those comic books. And thank you to my sister, Bari, for her super strength; to Noah Kuttler for his super hearing (and who pushed me so hard with this one); and to Teri Meltzer and Ben Rubin, my mother and Poppy, for giving me everything else I needed and in whose memory this project lives.

For me, this has never been just a book. It is a dream. So special thanks to Jill Kneerim, who shoved me along from the very first slumber; Hope Denekamp, Caroline Zimmerman, and everyone at the Kneerim & Williams Agency; my dear friend Larry Kirshbaum, the real godfather of this project; Simon Sinek, who told me my first inspiring story; Joel Marlin, who added the earliest research; Marie Grunbeck for reading my mind; Rusty Greiff and Elizabeth Shreve for sharing their sweet boy; Richard Mallory Allnutt for the cover photo; Katherine Blood from the Library of Congress; Chris Weiss, who inspired the first question; Rob Weisbach, the first to have faith; and all the real heroes who shared pictures and family stories.

A special thank you must also be said to my fellow dreamer and partner-in-crime, Brad Desnoyer, whose research made me really look like the history nerd I've always pretended to be. His contribution here cannot be overstated, but it's his friendship that is treasured.

Finally, a thank you to Katie Salisbury, Kathryn Ratcliffe-Lee, Debbie Stier, Jessica Wiener, Kim Lewis, Leah Carlson-Stanisic, Mary Schuck, Nikki Cutler, Doug Jones, and everyone at HarperStudio, for creating such a warm second home in the writing community. And to Bob Miller, for building that home so beautifully. I mean it, Bob. Thank you for this gift that I can give to my sons—and for your trust and faith.

introduction

I was stuck at a red light. It wasn't a particularly long light. But I remember the moment because it was dark and it was quiet—the first moment of quiet on the day my son Jonas was born.

And there I was, stuck at this red light.

It was one of those moments where you sit outside your body—like your first kiss, or that first time someone in your family dies—and you're looking down, knowing that the moment is so personally vital that the only way to comprehend it is to witness it from somewhere else.

So as I sat there, gripping the steering wheel of our little banged-up car, I remember looking up at the crisp black sky and thinking about this baby boy we were just blessed with. That's when it hit me—and when I asked myself the question for the very first time: what kind of man did I want my son to be?

I have three children now. I've long since realized I have little say in the matter.

But I still love that moment. That pure, beautiful moment where you get to think about your newborn child and every door and every possibility is just waiting there, perfectly open. You can dream as big as you want in that moment. That baby of yours may be the future president of the United States, or a creative genius, or a big thinker, or, best yet, the kind of person who leaves the world better than he found it.

It's a moment where there are no limits or detours or any of the restrictions that reality eventually brings. And it was in that moment of unbridled love and pure naïveté that this book was born.

I decided right there that I'd write this book over the course of my son's life—that I'd fill it with advice and good ideas. I started that very night, writing the instructions he needed to be a good man:

1. Love God.
2. Be nice to the fat kid in class.

The plan was that I'd add more ideas throughout his lifetime, and then one day, when he was older, he'd thank me, realizing what a brilliant father I was. (I'd assumed Cat Stevens would be playing in the background. Norman Rockwell would of course be resurrected to paint the moment.)

It was the day my son was born. I'm allowed mushy.

And so, on that day, I began this book.

Of course it was crap.

Sure, there was some good advice in there. But most of it was just sentimental manure—the ramblings of someone who clearly had never been a parent. I mean, did I really think that if I said, "Be good," my son would *be good*?

So I started thinking about my own life: Where did I learn kindness? Who taught me about the benefits of patience? I didn't have to look far. Sure, my mom and dad had laid the foundation. But when I thought of my first real hero, the person who came to mind was my grandfather, Ben Rubin.

When I was little, my grandfather knew I loved hearing Batman stories, so he'd always tell me this one story that went like this: "Batman and Robin were in the Batmobile. And they were riding along the edge of a curving cliff. And up ahead of them was a white van, which held the Joker, the Penguin, the Riddler, and Catwoman. And as they drove along this cliff, Batman and Robin *caught them*."

That's when I'd look him right in the eyes and whisper, "Tell it again."

He'd smile at me and say, "Batman and Robin were in the Batmobile. And they were riding along the edge of a curving cliff. . . . "

And when it was done, I'd say, "Tell it again."

And he would.

It was the same story every time. Just four sentences long. *Batman and Robin were in the Batmobile* . . . . But he told me this story over and over simply because he knew I loved hearing it.

That's a hero to me.

In that action, he taught me about love and compassion and dedication. He taught me the power of creativity. He opened the first window of my imagination. And most of all, as I look back on it, he showed me the true impact of a well-told story.

That's what I wanted for my son.

From there, I started looking for more heroes. I wanted to hear their stories—the ones no one knew. It made sense to me—especially since, as a parent, I know that the *only* lesson we ever teach is the one that comes from example.

One of the first stories I heard was about the Wright brothers. A friend told me that every day when Orville and Wilbur Wright went out to fly their plane, they would bring enough materials for multiple crashes. That way, when they crashed, they could rebuild the plane and try again. Think about it a moment: every time they went out— *every time*—they *knew* they were going to fail. But that's what they did: Crash and rebuild. Crash and rebuild. And that's why they finally took off.

I *loved* that story. I *still* love that story. And *that's* the kind of story I wanted my son to hear: a story that wouldn't lecture to him, but would show him that if he was determined . . . if he wasn't afraid to fail . . . if he had persistence (and a side order of stubbornness) . . . the impossible becomes possible.

Since that time, I've been collecting heroes and their stories for my son. (Though of course, every hero in here is heroic for both boys and girls alike. Every single one.)

There are thousands of heroes. And I think that's what I like best. There is proof—absolute proof—everywhere. Look around at any life and you'll find examples of charity and honesty, leadership and humility, tenacity and dignity. These are the tools I want my son to have. And the tools I want my daughter, Lila, to have. (I'm already working on her book.) Indeed, as this book got started, it became triply important: my younger son, Theo, was born. I want these tools for Theo too.

Does that mean every hero in the world is in here? Of course not. I purposely left out most religious leaders so there'd be no battling among faiths.

You'll see heroes you know, like Jim Henson and Eleanor Roosevelt. There are others who are not as well known, like Frank Shankwitz and Barbara Johns. And there are others who seem almost ridiculously obvious, like George Washington and Rosa Parks. But to be clear, this is not a book about fame. Thomas Jefferson isn't in here just because he wrote the Declaration of Independence. He's in here because he didn't publicize that fact (indeed, it didn't become common knowledge that he was the author until years after he was president), showing the kind of modesty that I want my sons to know about.

This isn't a book about how to be remembered—it's a book about how we live our lives, and what we are capable of on our very best days.

Is that schmaltzy and naive? I hope so. Because I want my sons to learn those things too.

We all are who we are—until that moment when we strive for something greater.

In the end, I suppose there are easier ways to share life's most valuable lessons with my sons. There were moments when I thought about doing it Mr. Miyagi style and teaching it through karate. But I don't know karate. And so I do the only thing I know how to do: I tell a story. Just like my grandfather taught me all those years ago.

BRAD MELTZER
Fort Lauderdale, Florida, 2009

heroes for
my son

the wright brothers

Inventors of the world's first flying machine.

When it was time to try building the first flying machine, Samuel Langley had incredible resources and tens of thousands in funding. Bicycle salesmen Orville and Wilbur Wright had a flying toy their father gave them as children and a dream they refused to give up on. Guess who won?

Every day, they knew they'd fail.

Every time they'd go out to fly—*every time*—they brought extra materials because they knew their fledgling design would crash.

Crash and rebuild. Crash and rebuild.

But never ever, ever give up. ★

If we worked on the assumption that what is accepted as true really is true, then there would be little hope for advance.

—Orville Wright

team hoyt

Father and son. Long-distance runners.

Although Rick Hoyt is profoundly disabled, he has competed with his father Dick in over one thousand marathons, triathlons, ironman competitions, and other long-distance events.

When Dick and Judy Hoyt's son was born with cerebral palsy, unable to walk or talk, the doctors told them to just "put him away."
No, they decided.
They'd push him, pull him, they'd carry him along.
But he'd never be left behind.

When the public schools said there was no place for Rick, his parents found a computer that would write his thoughts from the few head movements he could make.
At ten, he spoke his first sentence. "Go Bruins!"

In high school, Rick learned of a five-mile charity run for a newly paralyzed teenager.
Rick told his father they had to do something to send a message that life goes on.
Even though he wasn't a runner, Dick never hesitated.
He'd run the race, pushing Rick's wheelchair the whole way.

They finished next to last. It was a victory.
That night, Rick typed out these words: "Dad, when I'm running, it feels like my disability disappears."
Dick's mission was clear.
He kept running, Rick always out in front.
234 triathlons, 67 marathons, 6 ironmans.
Rick Hoyt still can't walk.
But with his father, they both fly. ★

Team Hoyt's motto: Yes you can.

joe shuster and jerry siegel

Inventors of the first superhero.

The creators of Superman—and Clark Kent—showed the world
that the most ordinary of us can turn out to be the most heroic.

They weren't good-looking.

They weren't popular.

And they were so poor that they used to draw on the back of butcher's paper.

But they were two best friends.

With one dream.

At the brink of World War II, in the midst of the Great Depression, two kids from Cleveland didn't just give us the world's first superhero.

They gave us something to believe in. ★

The trouble with this, kid, is that it's too sensational.
Nobody would believe it.

—One of the first rejection letters for *Superman*

mr. rogers

Television host of Mister Rogers' Neighborhood.

With little more than a cardigan and a friendly smile, Fred Rogers spent nearly forty years using public television to teach kindness—just *kindness*—to children. Did it work? After thieves stole Mr. Rogers's car, the story was broadcast on TV and in newspapers. The car was returned in two days.

The note in the car read: "If we'd known it was yours, we never would have taken it."

His parents were so worried about his hay fever, they kept him inside for an entire summer.

He had nothing to play with except for a toy piano and some homemade hand puppets.

Freddie made the best of it. He had his imagination.

He didn't need anything else. ★

Knowing that we can be loved exactly as we are gives us all the best opportunity for growing into the healthiest of people.

—Fred Rogers

When a bubble's gone, you don't see it anymore with your eyes. And when an opera is over, you don't hear it anymore with your ears. But you can remember it. You can remember what bubbles look like and what operas sound like and what friends feel like. And you'll always have them with you in your memory.

—Fred Rogers

miep gies

Found and preserved Anne Frank's diary.

Risking her life for those of her friends, Miep Gies protected eight people in a cramped annex—Otto Frank and his family of four, the Van Pels and their son, and an elderly dentist—from the Nazi death machine during World War II. After Anne and her family were discovered by the Germans and sent to Auschwitz, Miep, hoping that Anne would return, held on to the world's most important diary.

In the spring of 1942, Otto Frank asked his assistant the most important question of her life: "Are you prepared to help us?"

Miep Gies never hesitated. "Yes, of course," she said.

For two years, Miep broke the law—hiding and feeding eight people, including Otto's daughter, Anne.

When the Nazis burst in, Miep didn't deny helping the family.

She didn't apologize.

Instead, she tried to bribe Nazi officials into letting the eight innocent people go.

It didn't work.

And when the Nazis warned her not to return, Miep snuck back into the hiding spot.

Among the scattered papers and clothing, she noticed one thing the Nazis had dismissed—Anne's red-checked diary.

Never opening it, she placed it in a desk drawer.

When Anne's father returned after the war, Miep once again took him in.

When she heard that Anne was dead, Miep relinquished her duty as caretaker.

"Here," Miep told Otto, "is your daughter Anne's legacy to you." ★

I myself am just an ordinary woman. I simply had no choice.

—Miep Gies

roberto clemente

Baseball legend. Hometown hero.

Being one of the best baseball players in the world would satisfy most people. Roberto Clemente got better every year. As a right fielder with the Pittsburgh Pirates, he won twelve Gold Glove Awards and had the best batting average in four different seasons.

Being a baseball player made him famous.

Being a twelve-time Golden Glove winner made him rich.

So when an earthquake struck Nicaragua, he could have just written a check and gotten his name in the paper.

Instead, he got involved personally.

He funded three emergency relief flights.

All three were diverted by corrupt officials—which is why Clemente decided to fly on the fourth plane himself.

It was packed with as much food and medicine as he could possibly bring.

The plane crashed in the ocean, killing everyone on the flight.

But Roberto Clemente isn't a hero because the plane went down.

He's a hero because of why he got on board. ★

If you have a chance to accomplish something that will make things better for people coming behind you and you don't do that, you are wasting your time on this Earth.

—*Roberto Clemente*

He can run and throw—and we think he can hit.

—*Draft report on Roberto Clemente for the Pittsburgh Pirates*

amelia earhart

Record breaker. High-flying pilot.

A pioneer in aviation and the first female to cross the Atlantic, Amelia Earhart broke many flight records. She died while trying to become the first person to fly around the world at the equator. Her plane has still never been found.

She worked as a truck driver, stenographer, and photographer. Just to save enough for the flying lessons.

Six months after she learned to fly, she put away enough for a bright yellow, used biplane called *Canary*.

The following year, she broke her first record, reaching an altitude of fourteen thousand feet, the highest recorded at that time by a woman.

She wasn't a natural. She wasn't the best pilot.

She had to work at it.

But within her short lifetime she showed the world that the greatest flight we'll ever take is the one no one has tried before. ★

Please know I am quite aware of the hazards. . . . I want to do it because I want to do it. Women must try to do things as men have tried. When they fail their failure must be but a challenge to others.

—Amelia Earhart

Never interrupt someone doing what you said couldn't be done.

—Amelia Earhart

nelson mandela

President of South Africa, 1994 to 1999.

Under South African apartheid—the social and political policy of racial repression—activist Nelson Mandela was sent to prison for twenty-seven years. After his release, he negotiated the end of legal racial segregation in the country—and in 1994 became South Africa's president in the country's first free election.

Nelson Mandela was sent to work in the quarry.

Sent there so his will would be broken.

But deep in the mine, in what was supposed to be a latrine, he and the other prisoners created a school.

There the inmates became teachers of history and students of law, self-educated scholars preparing apartheid's end.

The men knew they could be punished for speaking.

They knew they could be punished for organizing.

Yet Mandela was arranging lectures on economics and politics, Sophocles and Shakespeare, readying the activists around him for the coming revolution.

In life, there are many prisons.

But even in the darkest ones, there are always possibilities. ★

In English, Nelson Mandela's given name, Rolihlahla, literally means "troublemaker."

norman borlaug

Father of the Green Revolution.

Norman Borlaug's brilliant mind allowed him to develop high-yielding, disease-resistant crops. He could have made millions. Instead, he devoted his life to saving others.

The lab produced camouflage, malaria repellents, and saltwater-proof glues for soldiers fighting in the South Pacific.

But after the war, Norman decided that he should use science for something other than fighting.

And so came the true birth of the Green Movement.

Norman Borlaug moved to Mexico and began doing manual labor in the wheat fields.

Working beside the farmers, he figured out how to grow more food.

Six times more.

He saved one million people from starvation in Mexico.

When he moved his family to India, he multiplied the region's grain output by fourfold and again saved a million lives.

By the time Norman came home, having worked on farms all over China and Africa, he had prevented one billion men, women, and children from dying of starvation—saving more people than anyone in human history. ★

You can't build a peaceful world on empty stomachs and human misery.

—Norman Borlaug

martin luther king jr.

Clergyman. Civil rights activist. Nobel Peace Prize winner.

At a time when it would've been so easy to use his fists, King embraced the path of peace—and in doing so, showed its true power. In his battle against hatred and racism, he died for his ideals. But most important, he lived for them.

The speech wasn't finished until 3:30 A.M. that morning. Yet on August 28, 1963, he was ready to take the podium.

FBI agents were stationed beside the PA system on the Washington Mall, ready to pull the plug at a moment's notice in case he said something incendiary.

And then, halfway through his text, Dr. King looked up from the printed page.

His written draft didn't include the words "I have a dream."

But it was when the young reverend stopped reading and started speaking that everyone heard.

No plug was pulled.

No dog attacked.

No fire hose was needed to control the crowd.

And though the president and Congress feared that a protest march would prevent the passage of civil rights legislation, they could have not been more wrong.

Nothing can stop a dream. ★

The hottest place in Hell is reserved for those who remain neutral in times of great moral conflict.

—Dr. Martin Luther King Jr.

anne sullivan

Teacher.

Helen Keller was deaf and blind from the age of one. With the help of her teacher Anne Sullivan, Helen became a prolific writer and activist.

No one believed that the deaf and blind girl would amount to anything. She was helpless.

At six years old, she couldn't speak, talk, or even eat with a fork.

But one teacher, who was nearly blind herself, had the patience to "finger-write" words into Helen's tiny hand.

Helen Keller was admitted to Radcliffe College, but the dean convinced her not to attend. Though the school had accepted her, he thought that college would be too much for her. But a year later, Helen was determined to try.

Since most of Helen's books couldn't be converted into Braille, Anne Sullivan spent five hours a day spelling onto Helen's hand the letters, the words, the sentences of the texts.

Straining to read the texts caused Anne's already-poor eyesight to deteriorate greatly. Anne's doctor warned—if she didn't stop reading to Helen, she'd risk going blind herself.

Anne kept on reading.

Helen Keller wrote her first book when she was just twenty-two years old. It was the first of fourteen books she would write.

And of course, thanks to her teacher, Anne Sullivan, Helen graduated from Radcliffe.

Cum laude. ★

Although the world is full of suffering, it is also full of the overcoming of it.

—Helen Keller

john lennon

Legendary singer-songwriter. Peace activist.

One of the founders of the Beatles, John Lennon created some of the world's most popular and complex songs. But his greatest impact wasn't on the pop charts. It was in his wartime songs: stubborn anthems advocating peace in Vietnam at a time when it would've been so much easier for him to stay quiet.

When John Lennon's Aunt Mimi told him music wasn't a job, he just kept playing on her porch.

When all he had was a cheap harmonica and a bus ticket, he played the entire way to Scotland.

And when that great moment came, when he had everyone listening, John Lennon led by example, singing about peace and redefining what a rock star can shout about.

By the time J. Edgar Hoover was tapping his phone and having him followed, John knew that there was only one way to deal with naysayers.

You just have to keep singing your song. ★

The guitar's all very well, John, but you'll never make a living out of it.

—John Lennon's Aunt Mimi

harriet tubman

Abolitionist. Union spy.

Selflessly leading southern slaves to freedom via the Underground Railroad, runaway slave Harriet Tubman became reverently known as "the Moses of her people." As she herself once stated, she "never lost a single passenger."

When Harriet Tubman escaped to the North, she was truly free.

Never again would she have to hold her breath in hidden rooms.

Never again would she have to lie perfectly still under false floors.

Never again would she have to dig holes to hide in swamps or sweet potato fields.

But she knew she had to go back.

In a time when there was big money to be made by catching runaway slaves, she risked her own capture over nineteen more trips, hiding by day, traveling by night, leading over three hundred people to their freedom.

It wasn't safe.

But it was right. ★

Every great dream begins with a dreamer.

—Harriet Tubman

harry houdini

Magician. Escapologist. Stunt artist.

Harry Houdini was the world's most famous
and accomplished escape artist. When he was
doing what he loved, nothing could hold him.

Though he knew it was honest work, the Weiss boy wanted out of the factory.

He tried to run away and join the circus, but after his father died, it fell on Ehrich to take care of his family.

Ten hours of cutting neckties . . . or ten hours sweeping in a carnival?

In the boardinghouse, they told him to take the work that's dependable.

Take the work that feeds your family.

Ehrich, however, had a vision.

He knew he walked a different path.

Flanked by bearded ladies and snake charmers, "the Great Houdini" stepped into the sideshow.

For almost a decade, he struggled to feed himself, his mother, his sister.

And then what began in a tent made its way to a theater.

Harry Houdini became the highest-paid vaudeville performer of his time, forever doing what he loved rather than what was safe. ★

My chief task has been to conquer fear.

—Harry Houdini

jackie robinson

Professional baseball player. Hall of Famer.

At a time when major league baseball was played only by whites, Jackie Robinson forever changed American sports by crossing baseball's sixty-year color line and becoming the first African American to play in the major leagues instead of the Negro leagues. He stole home nineteen times and was the National League Most Valuable Player in 1949, when he led in hitting (.342) and steals (37). With Robinson on their team, the Dodgers won six pennants in his ten seasons. He risked his life to do it.

Pitchers threw fastballs at his head.

Runners slid at him with their cleats.

Catchers spit on his shoes.

But it was from the stands that the hate letters and death threats came.

As a college student, Jackie had a reputation for fighting.

But not in the big leagues. There he practiced self-control.

Even when they warned that if he kept playing, they'd kidnap his son.

Even when his family waited by the radio, listening for gunshots.

Jackie kept silent, speaking loud with no words at all. ★

How you played in yesterday's game is all that counts.

—Jackie Robinson

albert einstein

The greatest scientist of his time.

Albert Einstein created the theory of relativity, won the Nobel Prize in Physics, and forever altered our understanding of the universe.

He didn't speak until he was three years old.

He was the worst-behaved kid in class.

When he was sick and bedridden in grade school, his father showed him a simple compass.

The compass fascinated the boy.

The needle's constant northern swing, guided by what seemed like an invisible force, convinced Einstein that there was "something behind things, something deeply hidden."

No one agreed.

One teacher called him a foolish dreamer and asked him to drop out.

But Einstein never stopped dreaming.

As an adult, he scribbled down his ideas and hid them in a desk drawer when his supervisors passed.

He went against conventional wisdom.

He questioned the status quo.

His idea? Everything is full of energy.

His conclusion? $E = mc^2$.

The theory of relativity didn't just change the world.

It showed us the universe. ★

The important thing is not to stop questioning. Curiosity has its own reason for existing. One cannot help but be in awe when he contemplates the mysteries of eternity, of life, of the marvelous structure of reality. It is enough if one tries merely to comprehend a little of this mystery every day. Never lose a holy curiosity.

—Albert Einstein

jesse owens

Gold medal winner. American hero.

Against Hitler's Aryan elites, Jesse Owens won four gold medals in track and field at the 1936 Berlin Olympics.

The swastika banners were hung everywhere.

Millions of Reichmarks were spent to fund the training of the blond, blue-eyed German athletes.

And in 1936 Berlin, from his lavish balcony, Adolf Hitler saluted his athletes with an outstretched arm, promising that, through sports, the world would finally see "Aryan superiority."

This was Hitler's Olympics.

Jesse Owens was the grandson of a slave, the son of a sharecropper. He suffered from bouts of pneumonia.

He bloomed as a runner. Colleges fought over him—but that didn't mean they thought he was equal.

At Ohio State, he was not offered a scholarship, even though he broke high school world records.

And unlike the Aryan supermen, Jesse Owens worked part-time just to eat.

Working as a gas station attendant, as a waiter, as a night elevator operator, at the campus library stacks—no one paid his way. Ever.

The German journalists and announcers wouldn't even use his name.

They said that "the Negro Owens" was a "nonhuman."

They thought the Aryan win was guaranteed.

Jesse Owens competed in four events at the 1936 Olympics.

He won the gold medal in all four.

And when he stood on the victory platform, surrounded by swastikas and soldiers, the German crowd of 110,000 couldn't help but cheer.

Rising to their feet, they were no longer chanting Hitler's name.

They were cheering for Jesse Owens. ★

One chance is all you need. —Jesse Owens

Upon returning to America, a ticker-tape parade was held in Jesse Owens's honor, but he was forced to ride the freight elevator to the reception at the Waldorf Astoria.

jim henson

Creator of Kermit the Frog and the Muppets.

Jim Henson was the voice of Kermit, Ernie, Rowlf, and Dr. Teeth. With the TV show *Sesame Street*, he taught and entertained generations of children simply by sharing—and believing in—his own idealistic dream.

He didn't set out to be a puppeteer. He just wanted to work in TV.

But at seventeen years old, when he went looking for a job at a local TV station, they rejected him.

While there, he saw a sign on a nearby bulletin board. The TV station was looking for a puppeteer.

Jim Henson went to the library, checked out a book on puppetry, built a few puppets, and returned to the station.

"Now I am a puppeteer. Will you hire me?"

They gave him five minutes.

It was all Jim Henson needed. ★

I've got a dream too, but it's about singing and dancing and making people happy. That's the kind of dream that gets better the more people you share it with.

—Kermit the Frog

But green's the color of spring
And green can be cool and friendly-like
And green can be big like an ocean
Or important like a mountain
Or tall like a tree.

—Kermit the Frog

jonas salk

Scientist and researcher.

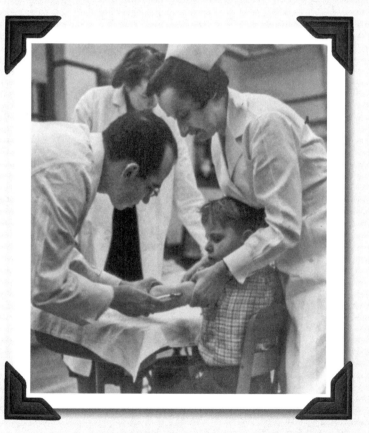

After working tirelessly for eight years, Jonas Salk
created a vaccine against polio.

It was an epidemic.
Children were becoming sick by the tens of thousands.
It terrified them. Paralyzed them. Broke their bodies.

Jonas Salk spent eight years searching for a way to prevent children from catching polio.
He worked sixteen-hour days, seven days a week.
Among the first people he tested his vaccine on were himself, his staff, and his wife and children.
Next came testing on one million children.

It was a success.

In 1955 America had its vaccine.
As payment, Jonas Salk could have asked for anything in the world.
He asked for nothing.

Edward R. Murrow asked him, "Who owns the patent on this vaccine?"
Salk simply replied, "Well, the people, I would say. There is no patent. Could you patent the sun?"

In 1952, 57,628 cases of polio were reported in the United States.
Today there are just over 1,500 cases worldwide.
None in the United States. ★

Great, we've made a great discovery!

—Jonas Salk's response whenever he was told in
the laboratory that something hadn't worked

dr. seuss

Author of The Cat in the Hat and other children's books.

Theodor Seuss Geisel wrote and illustrated *Green Eggs and Ham, Horton Hears a Who,* and forty-six other books that have entertained multiple generations. His secret? He's not like anyone else.

When Theodor Geisel realized that the current crop of children's books—stories like *Dick and Jane*—were *too nice*, he set out to change them.

Life magazine reported that those dull books were leading to massive literacy problems among kids.

So his publisher gave him 348 words not commonly read by schoolchildren but thought important to learn.

He took 223 words from the list and added 13 others. And with only those 236 words, he created a book 1,626 words in length.

He called it *The Cat in the Hat*.

It sold nearly one million copies within three years. Today over 200 million copies of Dr. Seuss books have been sold. ★

Unless someone like you cares a whole awful lot, nothing is going to get better. It's not.

—The Lorax by Dr. Seuss

Dr. Seuss's first children's book was rejected by twenty-seven different publishers.

bella abzug

Congresswoman. Defense attorney.
Leader of the women's rights movement.

A U.S. congresswoman from 1971 to 1976, Bella Abzug fought for the
withdrawal of troops from Vietnam, coauthored the Freedom of Information
Act, cosponsored the first World Conference on Breast Cancer, and, most
important, moved the fight for women's rights into the mainstream.

It was a disaster.
Willie McGee was a black man convicted of raping a white woman.
In Mississippi. In 1945. It didn't matter that he was innocent.
The jury deliberated for two and a half minutes before sentencing him to death.

Most people would've walked away from the case.
Most people would've known they couldn't overturn the conviction.
Luckily, Willie McGee didn't have most people for a lawyer.
He had Bella Abzug.

Eventually, all appeals were denied.
In the days before McGee's execution, the pregnant Abzug traveled to Jackson,
Mississippi, for a final hearing.
Her hotel wouldn't accept her reservation.
Neither would any other hotel in town.
She spent the night in a bathroom stall at the bus station to avoid the KKK.

Willie McGee was executed, and Bella Abzug suffered a miscarriage.

For most people, that would've been the end.
But as the next forty-seven years proved, as a member of Congress, as a feminist,
as a person who refused to walk away even when she probably should've, Bella
Abzug was just beginning to fight. ★

Women have been trained to speak softly and carry a lipstick. Those days are over.

*—Bella Abzug, who purposely never learned to
type in school so that she would never be seen as a secretary*

dan west

Relief worker. Farmer. Founder of Heifer International.

After seeing the devastation brought about by the Spanish Civil War in the late 1930s, Indiana farmer Dan West began sending livestock across the world to the poor and malnourished. His project continued, growing from his small idea to become Heifer International.

There wasn't enough powdered milk.

So every day, as a relief worker in the Spanish Civil War, Dan had to choose who would go hungry.

Every day he saw the same starving children.

And then Dan West thought of his healthy daughters back in Indiana. He thought of his farm. And he thought of a solution.

"Give them a cow, not a cup."

He started by sending seventeen cows to malnourished children in Puerto Rico. After World War II, more cows were sent to Europe and Japan then to poverty-stricken Africa and South America.

The only catch?

When each animal gave birth, the newborn animal had to go to another family.

The gift had to continue.

That's all Dan asked.

One man.

One idea.

Seventeen cows.

Today Heifer International has fed over 8.5 million people in 125 countries. ★

In all my travels around the world, the important decisions were made where people sat in a circle, facing each other as equals.

—Dan West

mother teresa

Volunteer. Relief worker. The Saint of the Gutters.

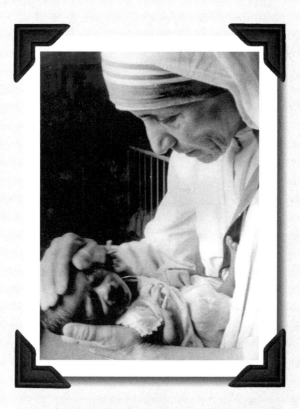

A simple nun who left the convent for the streets of Calcutta, Mother Teresa devoted her life to helping "the poorest of the poor." Most people thought she'd never make a difference.

On one of her first days in the slums, she had five rupees to her name. She gave four away to the poor.

Then a priest asked her for a donation, and her last rupee was gone.

Now she had nothing. She trusted in God to provide.

Later that same day, a benefactor who heard of her generosity came back to give her fifty rupees.

She gave those to the poor too.

When she needed medicine, she went to the pharmacist and said, "I need the medicines." The pharmacist laughed and moved on. Mother Teresa walked outside the pharmacy, got on her knees, and prayed. After several minutes the pharmacist brought out the medicine.

At the time of her death, the five-foot-tall nun who gave away her first five rupees had become the inspiration for 4,000 nuns who ran nearly 600 orphanages, homeless shelters, soup kitchens, and clinics in over 120 countries.

Since her death, the impact of Missionaries of Charity has not declined.

It's grown. ★

Do not wait for leaders. Do it alone. Person to person.

—Mother Teresa

steven spielberg

Director. Producer. Philanthropist.

Perhaps the most influential filmmaker in history, Steven Spielberg is responsible for some of the biggest movies to hit the silver screen—as well as some of the most vital.

E.T.
Raiders of the Lost Ark
Jurassic Park
Jaws
The Color Purple
Schindler's List
Saving Private Ryan

He is arguably the most famous, most successful, most admired director to ever work in film.

But the most important movies he's ever made are ones that the fewest number of people will see: the nearly fifty-two thousand videotaped testimonies from Holocaust survivors and other witnesses.

In 1994, in response to the success of *Schindler's List*, Steven Spielberg established the Shoah Foundation to ensure that the atrocities committed during the Holocaust could never be denied.

The work of the foundation will last far longer than big numbers at the box office. ★

Our hope is that the archive will be a resource so enduring that ten, or fifty, or even one hundred years from now people around the world will learn directly from survivors and witnesses about the atrocities of the Holocaust.

—*Steven Spielberg*

george h.w. bush

Pilot. Navy man. U.S. president.

Before he was president, before he was the director of the CIA, George H. W. Bush was an eighteen-year-old flyboy, America's youngest naval aviator at the time. During World War II, he piloted fifty-eight ultra-hazardous missions.

"Hit the silk! Hit the silk!" the twenty-year-old pilot yelled to his crew, signaling for them to bail from the smoking plane.

He knew what would happen if they were captured: torture and decapitation.

The plane was a fireball, falling from the sky.
Still, he was determined to save his crewmen, John Delaney and Ted White.
He maneuvered starboard to take the slipstream pressure off the crew's door.
It was the one way to give them a better chance to survive.

He gave them enough time to get out first.
But when his parachute opened too early, George Bush's head rammed into the bomber's tail.

When he landed, he was bleeding, vomiting, crying.
He'd just survived a burning plane crash.
His crewmates, despite all his actions, didn't.

His crewmates didn't just give their lives.
They gave him a reason to appreciate living.

It is a gift George Bush has never forgotten: "This is for Ted White and John Delaney. Here we go. . . ." ★

God bless those boys.

—George H. W. Bush

lucille ball

Actor. Trailblazer.

The star and creative force behind the early TV show *I Love Lucy*, Lucille Ball became the greatest comedian of her time and one of the most beloved entertainers ever—solely through her ability to find a laugh in what everyone else was taking so seriously.

She was sent to live with Grandmother Peterson.
Grandmother Peterson believed happiness was a sin.

In her house, mirrors were banned—except the one in the bathroom—since they led to vanity.

Instead, Lucy would play in the chicken coop, pretending it was her castle, the chickens her loyal army.
For friends? Lucy created one: "Sassafrassa."

Only Sassafrassa gave Lucy compliments, telling Lucy she was far more beautiful than Grandmother knew.
Lucy needed to hear it. If she was caught looking in a mirror, she was punished.

This was the girl who relished the chance to see her own reflection.
Contorting her face and widening her eyes in trolley car windows, she loved to see the possibilities. The simple humor of it.

And as she proved to the world, that humor could take on anything. ★

Love yourself first and everything falls into line.

—Lucille Ball

Between 1952 and 1953, when TV studio executives thought no one would watch the wacky redhead and her Cuban husband, on a typical Monday night two out of three households with TV sets proved them wrong.

george washington

General. Leader. First president.

As the commander of the Continental Army, George
Washington won the Revolutionary War. As president of
the United States, he won the world's admiration.

He'd won.

He'd led farmers and fishermen in a battle against the greatest fighting force in the world.

And he'd won.

At that moment—at the height of his popularity—George Washington could have easily declared himself king of America. The people would have followed. He could've held power for the rest of his life.

Back in England, the defeated King George III asked what Washington's plans were.

"They say he will return to his farm," the American painter Benjamin West replied.

"If he does that," King George said, "he will be the greatest man in the world."

And that's what Washington did.

And he did it again when he left the presidency after his second term.

It was the greatest, most heroic act of his career: putting his faith, not just in his country, but in us. ★

Few men have virtue to withstand the highest bidder.

—George Washington

charlie chaplin

Director. Actor. Silent film star.

The instantly recognizable **"Little Tramp"** of silent film, Charlie Chaplin turned the experiment called movies into a legitimate art form.

When Charlie was seven years old, his mother suffered from hallucinations and migraine headaches so severe that she could no longer care for him and his brothers.

There was only one choice, the doctors decided: She was sent to a psychiatric hospital.

Eventually, they let her out.

When Charlie was fourteen, she went back to the asylum.

His mother had been knocking on front doors, handing out pieces of coal, and insisting they were birthday presents.

She complained of seeing the dead staring at her.

Desperate to stay out of the workhouse, Charlie slept in alleyways, ate from garbage cans, and stole food.

To this day, historians argue about whether or not Chaplin based his most famous character—his Little Tramp—on his own life.

It doesn't matter.

Within months of the character's debut, Chaplin was the biggest film star in the world.

The money came quick.

He could afford anything he wanted.

The first thing he did after making his first full-length feature was buy a house in California and hire a nursing staff for his mom. ★

Failure is unimportant. It takes courage to make a fool of yourself.

—Charlie Chaplin

oprah winfrey

Talk show host. Influence maker. Businesswoman.

In 1983 Oprah Winfrey was given a local Chicago-area talk show to host. It was dead last in the ratings. Then it became an internationally syndicated phenomenon.

Maybe it was the poverty—wearing potato sacks as dresses and keeping cockroaches as pets.

Maybe it was running away from an abusive home, with no one to help her.

Or maybe it was being told by her bosses to get plastic surgery, since her eyes were too far apart, her nose was too flat, and her hair was too "black."

It could have been any of these experiences. Or all of them.

But somewhere along the way, the little girl with so much drive, the little girl who loved to talk, the one they used to call "the Preacher," came to a conclusion.

She teaches it every day. And we love her because even she's still learning it: The only person you ever need to be is yourself. ★

Do the one thing you think you cannot do. Fail at it. Try again. Do better the second time. The only people who never tumble are those who never mount the high wire.

—Oprah Winfrey

officer frank shankwitz

Cofounder of the Make-A-Wish Foundation.

Highway patrolman Frank Shankwitz cofounded the Make-A-Wish Foundation after he saw what a day of escape could mean to a child with a life-threatening medical condition. Thanks to Frank's vision, a wish is now granted every forty minutes.

It started with a boy named Chris Greicius.
Chris wanted to be a police officer.
The problem was, he had leukemia. He was dying.

But when Chris met Officer Frank Shankwitz, when he saw Shankwitz's motorcycle, and when Shankwitz came to the boy's home and created a toy-motorcycle riding test, for just that day Chris forgot about the leukemia eating away at his body.

Two days after the visit, Chris was in a coma.
Shankwitz went to the boy's hospital room to present him with real "motorcycle wings."
When he pinned them on the boy's uniform, young Chris actually came out of the coma.
And smiled.

On the flight back from Chris's funeral, Shankwitz had an idea.
What if he could somehow give that same joy to other kids like Chris . . . just for one day?
Right there, the Make-A-Wish Foundation was born. ★

I am still amazed and inspired how one little boy's dream to be a policeman has touched the lives of so many thousands of people.

—Linda Bergandahl-Pauling, mother of Chris Greicius

mark twain

Humorist. Novelist. Storyteller.

The author of *The Adventures of Huckleberry Finn*, Mark Twain was the greatest humorist in American history. More important, he used his abilities as a fiction writer to share his convictions with the world.

People thought they were reading something funny.

They thought it'd give them a taste of the deep South.

They thought they were getting the local color along the Mississippi River.

They thought *Huckleberry Finn* was just some story about a boy.

And it was.

But it was also a manifesto.

A challenge.

An uncompromising fistfight against injustice and slavery.

People thought they were getting a book.

But Mark Twain knew that if you really want to teach people something, you need to tell them a story. ★

Keep away from people who try to belittle your ambitions. Small people always do that, but the really great make you feel that you, too, can become great.

—Mark Twain

Always do right. This will gratify some people and astonish the rest.

—Mark Twain

eleanor roosevelt

Activist. Role model. Wife of President Franklin Delano Roosevelt.

The first lady during the Great Depression and World War II,
Eleanor Roosevelt became a fighter for women's rights,
minorities' rights, and social justice.

In 1932, seventeen thousand veterans and their families descended on Washington, D.C., and built a tent city, demanding what they believed were overdue payments for their service during World War I.

President Hoover sent General Douglas MacArthur and troops armed with fixed bayonets to meet the veterans with force. With tanks. With tear gas.

By March 1933, when the veterans returned, FDR was president. Instead of sending the Army, he sent his wife, Eleanor Roosevelt.

The first lady went to the tent city. Alone.

In mud and rain, she walked among the veterans. She talked to them like people. She listened.

Soon after, an executive order was issued that created twenty-five thousand jobs for veterans through the Civilian Conservation Corps and eventually led to the 1944 passage of the GI Bill of Rights, which gave veterans federal assistance in returning to civilian life. ★

No one can make you feel inferior without your consent.

—Eleanor Roosevelt

Many journalists suggested that if Eleanor Roosevelt wanted to comment on politics, she should do it off the record. That wasn't her way.

"I am making these statements on purpose," she said, "to arouse controversy and thereby get the topics talked about."

Race relations, the suffrage movement, poverty—every topic was fair game. Indeed, President Roosevelt didn't publicly support civil rights for black people—until after the first lady started speaking out against the social injustice of Jim Crow laws.

neil armstrong

Test pilot. Astronaut. Space traveler.

On July 20, 1969, *Apollo 11* mission commander Neil
Armstrong became the first person to set foot on the
moon, embodying the hopes and dreams of generations.

At ten, he started cutting grass at the cemetery, just so he could earn enough money to buy that model plane.
But a model wouldn't cut it.

At fifteen, he worked three jobs at forty cents an hour, saving it all to pay for flying lessons.
But lessons could only take him so far.

At sixteen, when his friends were learning to drive, he earned his pilot's license.
Then he hitched a ride home to tell his parents.
But he still didn't have a plane.

At thirty, he fearlessly tested two hundred different aircraft.
The X-15 rocket plane went faster and higher than any plane had gone before.
But it wasn't fast enough.

At thirty-nine, he floated down the ladder, his voice calm, his movements unhurried.
Then he took a small step . . . and began walking on the moon.

Still, Neil Armstrong was being modest.
It wasn't just *one small step* that got him there.
It was the thousands that came before it. ★

I think we're going to the moon because it's in the nature of the human being to face challenges.

—*Neil Armstrong*

paul newman

Actor. Sex symbol. Philanthropist.

Founder of the *Newman's Own* food line and benefactor of numerous philanthropic causes, actor Paul Newman used his fame to help others.

It started the week before Christmas 1980.

He mixed the first big batch of salad dressing in his basement, stirring the tub with a canoe paddle.

They poured it into wine bottles and put ribbons on them.

He thought it'd be fun. Then it got serious.

Even if it didn't work, all the profits were going to charity, so at least there'd be a little bit more for cancer research.

Dressings, popcorns, salsas, and $265 million later, movie star Paul Newman proved that true success doesn't come from getting—it comes from giving.

To this day, larger companies regularly approach Newman's Own, offering to acquire it. These offers are—always—politely refused. ★

> *A man with no enemies is a man with no character.*
>
> —Paul Newman

> *I'd like to be remembered as a guy who tried—tried to be part of his times, tried to help people communicate with one another, tried to find some decency in his own life, tried to extend himself as a human being. Someone who isn't complacent, who doesn't cop out.*
>
> —Paul Newman

pelé

Soccer superstar. Natural athlete. Worldwide phenomenon.

Brazilian soccer superstar Edison Arantes do Nascimento—better known as Pelé—is one of the greatest athletes the modern world has ever known. According to *Time* magazine, "He scored an average of a goal in every international game he played—the equivalent of a baseball player's hitting a home run in every World Series game over 15 years."

Scoring is great.

Blocking is great.

Winning is great.

But none of those equals *greatness*.

In 1967 the Nigerian civil war came to a sudden halt.

For forty-eight hours the two sides—so determined to murder each other—called a ceasefire.

They hadn't reached a moment of understanding.

They just wanted to watch Pelé play his exhibition match in the Nigerian capital of Lagos.

When the match was over, they would go back to violence and murder.

But for forty-eight hours, they would all stand together—just to witness this one man's God-given gift.

To witness greatness. ★

Success is no accident. It is hard work, perseverance, learning, studying, sacrifice, and most of all, love of what you are doing or learning to do.

—Pelé

barbara johns

High school student. Civil rights activist.

In 1951, sixteen-year-old Barbara Johns organized a walkout from her all-black high school. It led to *Brown v. Board of Education* and the end of public school segregation.

In 1951 Barbara Johns's school held 450 black students, all of them crowded into a building meant for 200.
Their books were tattered. Their classrooms had no heat.

One morning, when she missed her bus, she waited, hoping another might come.
Another did.
But it blew right by her, filled with white kids, heading to their newer, less crowded school.
As the bus disappeared, Barbara decided she'd organize a walkout.

Before Rosa Parks and Martin Luther King Jr., the early civil rights movement relied a great deal on the power of normal, unknown teenagers.
Teenagers.

Thanks to sixteen-year-old Barbara Johns, Moton High School held a two-week strike.
The NAACP helped them sue for an integrated school.
And it became one of the five cases that the Supreme Court reviewed when it declared segregation unconstitutional in *Brown v. Board of Education*.

For her reward, Barbara's house was burned down.
She never regretted it. ★

We knew we had to do it ourselves and that if we had asked for adult help before taking the first step, we would have been turned down.

—*Barbara Johns*

aung san suu kyi

Political captive. Leader of Burma's democratic movement.

Burmese opposition leader Aung San Suu Kyi has devoted her life to the freedom of the Burmese people. For peacefully advocating a nonviolent struggle over a military dictatorship, she won the Nobel Peace Prize in 1991. The repressive government of Burma has kept her in detention for much of the time since 1989. She still won't give up.

With a crowd of 500,000 watching her, Aung San Suu Kyi seized the microphone.
She was just a housewife. She had never held political office.
All she wanted was freedom—true democracy—for her beloved country of Burma.
Her plan? That was the surprise.
She stuck to one principle: nonviolent demonstration.

The brutal Burmese leaders reacted by killing hundreds and crushing the pro-democracy rallies.
Suu Kyi's response was the same. Peace.

They placed her under house arrest without charges or a trial.
When her pro-democracy party won the first Burmese elections held in thirty years, making her the rightful prime minister, the junta ignored the results.
When photographs of her began to suddenly appear on street corners, Suu Kyi's very image was banned.
And when they offered her a way out—her freedom in return for leaving the country—Suu Kyi refused. She would never leave Burma. Not until it was free. Even if that meant she never would be.

She never fought with force. But she never backed down.

In 2003 Suu Kyi was again placed under house arrest.
She's still there.
Over fourteen years of detention so far.
She has the key—all she has to do is leave. Behave.
Some people just don't know how. ★

In physical stature she is petite and elegant, but in moral stature she is a giant.
Big men are scared of her. Armed to the teeth and they still run scared.

—Archbishop Desmond Tutu

eli segal

Businessman. Political strategist. Optimist.

As the founding CEO of the Corporation for National Service, Eli Segal helped
launch AmeriCorps, President Clinton's national service program. Along the way,
through his sense of humor and genuine kindness, he inspired a generation of
young people to ask what they could do to leave this country a better place.

It's not because he helped establish AmeriCorps, enabling over 500,000 young people to do community service across our country.

It's not because he transformed millions of lives through his leadership on the Welfare-to-Work Partnership.

It's not because he fought so bravely against the cancer that killed him.

It's not even because he helped elect a president.

It's simply because, when I was twenty-one years old and he was running a small business in Boston, Eli Segal took a chance on me—his overenthusiastic intern—and offered me my very first grown-up job.

He knew I was too young. He used to lie about my age to people we would meet with.

But he believed in young people. And he believed in me. ★

THE AMERICORPS PLEDGE

I will get things done for America to make our people safer, smarter, and healthier.
I will bring Americans together to strengthen our communities.
Faced with apathy, I will take action.
Faced with conflict, I will seek common ground.
Faced with adversity, I will persevere.
I will carry this commitment with me this year and beyond.
I am an AmeriCorps member . . . and I am going to get things done.

I was just thinking all over again what an astonishing human being he was.

—*President Bill Clinton*

abraham lincoln

Lawyer. Senator. President.

One of America's greatest leaders, Abraham Lincoln lost eight elections. Despite those defeats, he became the sixteenth president of the United States and held the country together during the bloodshed of the Civil War.

Today there is a phrase for it: political suicide.

It's what happens when you say something that most people disagree with.

In 1858, while Abraham Lincoln was trying to get elected to the United States Senate, Stephen Douglas represented "most people."

Douglas said that blacks had no rights.

He said that the promise of life, liberty, and the pursuit of happiness did not apply to them.

The Supreme Court of the United States agreed.

But Abraham Lincoln didn't.

Lincoln stood up.

Lincoln spoke his mind.

And Lincoln lost.

He was sent home with nothing.

It *was* political suicide.

But it was worth it. ★

I am not bound to win, but I am bound to be true. I am not bound to succeed, but I am bound to live by the light that I have. I must stand with anybody that stands right, and stand with him while he is right, and part with him when he goes wrong.

—Abraham Lincoln

andy miyares

Special Olympics swimmer.

Born with Down's syndrome, Andy Miyares has used the water as a place to train his muscles and his mind. As a Special Olympics swimmer, he is unstoppable.

Andy Miyares was born with Down's syndrome.

At nine months old, because of a lack of muscle control, he couldn't sit up, and he couldn't crawl.

But his parents had an idea—swimming.

The doctors said Andy wouldn't walk until he was three years old.

He proved them wrong at thirteen months.

He learned math by counting laps.

Social skills from competing in meets.

At eight, he entered Special Olympics.

At twenty-one, he swam the San Francisco Bay.

And at twenty-three, he was invited to the Special Olympics World Summer Games.

Andy's hands and feet are the size of a five-year-old's; his height only five-feet-one-inch tall.

Even in the Special Olympics, people assume he's an underdog.

But he's earned fifteen world records. ★

I am not different from you.

—*Andy Miyares*

clara hale

Foster mother. Harlem resident. The heart of Hale House.

Clara Hale turned a Harlem brownstone into a refuge. For over twenty years, she cared for infants born suffering from drug withdrawals and HIV/AIDS. For those children—and all the people who joined in to help—Hale House was proof of the power of one person.

She started with the foster kids, raising forty of them, eight at a time, in her Harlem residence.

At sixty-three years of age, Clara Hale thought she was done.

Then came the drug-addicted mother with the two-year-old falling from her arms. Clara couldn't refuse.

Soon, twenty-two infants of drug-addicted parents were in Clara's five-room apartment.

City officials weren't impressed. Despite her 90 percent success rate, they tried to shut her down.

It didn't stop Hale House. Or Clara.

People started sending their own money—like the Englishman who called, looking for the "old lady of Harlem." It was John Lennon. He gave her $10,000.

Clara kept taking them in: children born addicted to crack, those dying of AIDS, the ones no one else wanted.

When she died at eighty-seven, Clara had helped raise almost one thousand children of every race and ethnicity.

She didn't have money.
She didn't have power.
Clara Hale had love.
It was endless. ★

Go to her house some night, and maybe you'll see her silhouette against the window as she walks the floor talking softly, soothing a child in her arms—Mother Hale of Harlem.

—Ronald Reagan

muhammad ali

Boxer. Prognosticator. Personality.

Muhammad Ali's grace and tenacity, combined with his rope-a-dope style, made him the undisputed heavyweight champion of boxing. He didn't just fight boxers, though. He took on the U.S. government, which charged him for refusing to serve in Vietnam. But what made him most powerful was his unbridled pride in himself.

No one floated faster.

No one stung harder.

No one taunted louder.

And no one—black or white, activist or athlete—brought more beauty, grace, or personality.

But what made him the greatest?

He never—*ever*—apologized for being who he was. ★

Champions aren't made in the gyms. Champions are made from something they have deep inside them—a desire, a dream, a vision.

—Muhammad Ali

I hated every minute of training, but I said, "Don't quit. Suffer now and live the rest of your life as a champion."

—Muhammad Ali

barack obama

President.

The journey of Barack Obama, the forty-fourth president of the United States of America, is just beginning, but even his critics acknowledge the amazing story of everything it took to arrive at the White House.

What do you call the son of a Kenyan economist and a girl from Kansas?

A black boy raised by white grandparents in a cramped two-bedroom apartment in Hawaii?

A rebellious student who scooped ice cream at Baskin-Robbins?

An idealistic college graduate searching to make a difference?

A law professor still struggling to make peace with the memory of his father?

A senator who favored the power of *hope*, igniting generations of believers?

You call him proof that, in America, anyone can be president. ★

I will never forget that the only reason I'm standing here today is because somebody, somewhere stood up for me when it was risky. Stood up when it was hard. Stood up when it wasn't popular. And because that somebody stood up, a few more stood up. And then a few thousand stood up. And then a few million stood up. And standing up, with courage and clear purpose, they somehow managed to change the world.

—Barack Obama

harper lee

Author of To Kill a Mockingbird.

In 1960 Harper Lee's first and only novel began influencing readers' perceptions of race and innocence. It is perhaps the most celebrated American novel of the twentieth century.

She didn't think the story was there.

Five years after starting, she was convinced her novel wasn't worth a damn.

Maybe she should've become a lawyer after all.

It was then that she threw open her window and tossed the manuscript out, scattering it in the filthy snow.

In a fit, Harper Lee called her editor Tay Hohoff. No one knows what Hohoff said to her.

But when Harper Lee hung up, she went outside, gathered the pages, and saved the manuscript.

She revised and revised and revised—until *To Kill a Mockingbird* was ready. ★

I think there's just one kind of folks. Folks.

—Scout

According to the Library of Congress, To Kill a Mockingbird *is second only to the Bible in being most often cited as making a difference in people's lives.*
    It is the only novel Harper Lee ever published.

thomas jefferson

Author of the Declaration of Independence.
Thinker. Statesman. President.

Thomas Jefferson was delegated by the Continental Congress to write a document proclaiming the colonies free from British rule. His Declaration of Independence became America's first words.

For seventeen days, the thirty-three-year-old secluded himself in a rented room in Philadelphia.

On a small, portable desk, he began writing, laying the foundations of this new American government. Unlike every nation before it, this country's heart would not beat with the blood of royal lines. This would be a nation based on ideals.

It took Thomas Jefferson seventeen days to find the right words.

Seventeen days of writing and rewriting before he nervously presented his document to John Adams and Benjamin Franklin.

The Declaration of Independence became the greatest decree in Western civilization.

Jefferson could've easily taken credit for writing it. But he never bragged about his accomplishment. Even when he was elected president, most Americans never knew he was the author of their independence.

In fact, his authorship didn't become common knowledge until years later after his death.

Because to Jefferson, the Declaration of Independence was written not just *for* all of America, but *by* all of America. It was the manifestation of a new nation and a new mind.

He was merely the messenger. ★

In matters of style, swim with the current; in matters of principle, stand like a rock.

—Thomas Jefferson

mahatma gandhi

Spiritual leader. Political icon. Pacifist.

Through nonviolent civil disobedience, political and spiritual leader Mohandas Gandhi united India in a struggle for independence. Known as Mahatma—"The Great Soul"—he fought for religious tolerance, economic self-sufficiency, and the end of British rule over his country. He went to prison. He fasted. He preached. But Gandhi never raised his hand in anger. It worked.

One day, you will fight.

So how should you fight?

With your fists? With threats? With words? With weapons?

They all work. They've been tested—successfully—for centuries.

But to fight by purposely avoiding violence?

To refuse to raise your fist, no matter what is raised against you?

Some would call that *lunacy*.

Madness.

But what it really is, is *courage*. ★

In a gentle way, you can shake the world.

—Gandhi

Whenever you are confronted with an opponent, conquer him with love.

—Gandhi

frederick douglass

Abolitionist. Speaker. Teacher.

Frederick Douglass escaped from slavery at the age of twenty. In his speeches and books, he became one of America's foremost orators, teaching whites, blacks, and an entire nation about the injustice of slavery, while also fighting for equality for all people.

Some arm themselves with guns.
Some with knives.
Some with bombs.

Born into slavery, Frederick Douglass armed himself with something far more dangerous.
His masters whipped him for it.
They used a hickory stick to beat him over the head.
They starved him until he collapsed.
But none of those punishments stopped him from finding it—the greatest, most powerful weapon ever created:

The ability to read.
And the bravery to share his story.

At sixteen, Frederick Douglass began teaching—illegally showing slaves how to read and write.
By twenty, he'd escaped to New York, where he found an even larger audience.

In the end, the other side had power.
Frederick Douglass just had words.

They didn't stand a chance. ★

If there is no struggle, there is no progress.

—Frederick Douglass

chesley b. sullenberger III

Pilot. Superbly disciplined.

When the engines went dead, Captain Chesley Sullenberger kept his calm and saved 155 lives by gently landing US Airways Flight 1549 in the Hudson River.

It's one thing to have all the piloting experience, to know what to do when both engines on the airplane fail, to take an Airbus that's not designed for gliding and do exactly that because you're also a certified glider pilot.

It's another thing to take all that experience and, as the plane is plummeting from the sky, still remain completely calm.

And it's yet another thing—while the plane is sinking in the Hudson River and drifting with the current—to walk the aisle of the cabin, making sure all the passengers get out before you do.
And then to walk that aisle again, just to be sure.

But when it was all finished and every TV camera came to your front door—to humbly shrug and say you were just doing your job?

That wasn't just bravery.
That was honor. ★

SULLENBERGER:
We're going to be in the Hudson.

AIR TRAFFIC CONTROL:
I'm sorry—say again, Captain?

One way of looking at this might be that for forty-two years I've been making small, regular deposits in this bank of experience: education and training. And on January 15 the balance was sufficient so that I could make a very large withdrawal.

—Chesley Sullenberger

rosa parks

Mother of the civil rights movement.

On a crowded bus in 1955, African American seamstress Rosa Parks refused to give up her seat to a white man. Her act of defiance ignited the Montgomery Bus Boycott, which lasted 381 days. Then public busing segregation came to an end. And a movement began.

Yes, she was tired.

She had grown up with the KKK riding past her house, her grandfather standing guard with the shotgun.

She had endured seeing her school burn down—twice.

She had faced this bus driver before, when he left her to walk five miles in the rain because she sat down in the white section to pick up her purse.

She had lived with injustice her entire life.

Yes, she was tired.

But it wasn't the kind of *tired* that came from aching feet.

"The only tired I was was tired of giving in."

So when the bus driver motioned to her to stand and give her seat away to a white person, the seamstress from Montgomery, Alabama, refused.

"Well, I'm going to have you arrested," the bus driver said.

Rosa Parks calmly replied, "You may go on and do so."

For violating Chapter 6, Section 11, of the Montgomery City Code, Rosa Parks went to jail.

For standing up for herself—by sitting down—Rosa Parks ignited a movement. ★

All I was doing was trying to get home from work.

—Rosa Parks

lou gehrig

Baseball legend. World's best first baseman. Ironman.

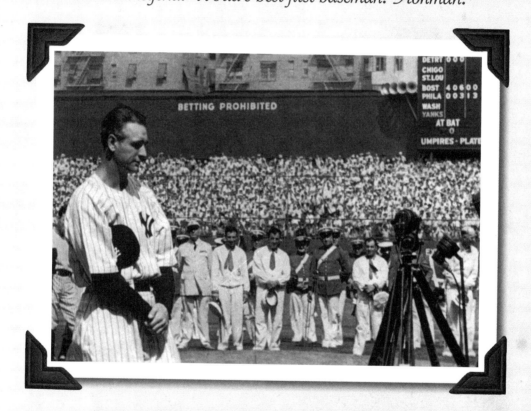

Despite muscle spasms and broken bones, New York Yankee Lou Gehrig played in 2,130 consecutive games. In thirteen of those seasons, he scored 100 runs and hit 100 RBI. His batting average of .361 in seven World Series brought the Yankees six titles. It took a debilitating and fatal disease to take him off the field, and even then he wasn't beat.

For thirteen seasons, Lou Gehrig never missed a single game.
Think of it.
Think of what happens over thirteen years.

He didn't miss a game when he was sick.
Or when he was tired, or bored, or not feeling right.

Not when he was under the weather, or drained, or just wanted to take a day for himself.

Not when he broke his thumb.
Or his toe.
Or when he suffered the seventeen other "healed" fractures that they found in just his hand and that they never knew about because he never complained.

For thirteen seasons, for more than two thousand games in a row,
Lou Gehrig showed up,
because he never wanted to let us down.

The only thing that stopped him?
The fatal disease that once caused his back to spasm so badly, he had to be carried off the field.

They called Lou Gehrig "the Iron Horse."
But he wasn't made of iron.
He was made like us.

He just didn't let that stop him. ★

I consider myself the luckiest man on the face of the Earth. And I might have been given a bad break, but I've got an awful lot to live for.

—Lou Gehrig, farewell speech, July 4, 1939, Yankee Stadium

teri meltzer

My mom.

It was the worst day of my professional life.

My publisher was shutting down, and we had no idea if another publisher would take over my contract.

This was terrifying to me. I was wracked with fear, feeling like I was watching my career deteriorate.

But as I shared my fears with my mother, her reaction was instantaneous: "I'd love you if you were a garbage man."

It wasn't anything she practiced. It was just her honest feelings at that moment.

To this day, *every* day that I sit down to write, I say those words to myself—"I'd love you if you were a garbage man"—soaking in the purity and selflessness of that love from my mother.

Her name was Teri Meltzer. And, Theo, she's the woman you're named after. ★

Now you'll understand how I love you.

—Teri Meltzer, on the birth of each of my children

Not everyone is nice like that.

—The receptionist in my mom's doctor's office,
when she heard that my mom had died from breast cancer.
Always remember: the truth is what people say behind your back.

ben rubin

My grandfather.

He was bald.

He had flat feet.

And he was just a cutter, spending long days slicing fabrics in the garment center.

But he was my grandfather.

Your great-grandfather.

And when I was your age, he used to tell me stories about Batman, simply because he knew how much I loved Batman stories.

He made up those stories just for me, inspiring me to be a writer.

Which is why, Jonas Benjamin, I named you after him. ★

He sounds nice.

—Jonas Benjamin Meltzer, age six

your hero's
photo here

your hero's story here . . .

_____

_____

_____

_____

_____

_____

_____

_____

_____

_____

_____

_____

_____

_____

There are many heroes in this world. Far more than we could fit in one book. If you have a hero, please share your story with us. Your hero could be someone everyone knows or someone only you know. We'd love to hear, for instance, about the teacher or mentor who made a difference in your life.

So please send your story to:

brad@heroesformyson.com

or to

Brad Meltzer
20533 Biscayne Boulevard, #371
Aventura, FL 33180

To see even more of what you can do, please visit:
www.OrdinaryPeopleChangeTheWorld.com
and
www.HeroesForMySon.com.

Photograph Credits

Grateful acknowledgment is given to the following sources for photographs in this book:

Jacket photograph © Richard Mallory Allnutt 2008, www.rmallnutt.com

Neil Armstrong © NASA Johnson Space Center Collection, George H. W. Bush © George Bush Presidential Library, Roberto Clemente © Jim Hanson, Clara Hale © Hale House, Jim Henson © Bernard Gotfryd, Barbara Johns © Robert Russa Moton Museum, Teri Meltzer and Ben Rubin © Brad Meltzer, Andy Miyares © Miyaris Family/Special Olympics Florida, Jackie Robinson © National Baseball Hall of Fame Library, Cooperstown, NY, Eleanor Roosevelt © Franklin D. Roosevelt Presidential Library, Eli Segal © Phyllis Segal, Officer Frank Shankwitz © Frank Shankwitz/Make-A-Wish Foundation, Team Hoyt © Team Hoyt Foundation, Dan West © Heifer International, Oprah Winfrey © Charlie Knoblock/Associated Press

Corbis Images: Paul Newman © Bettmann, Barack Obama © Obama for America/Reuters, Steven Spielberg © Steve Schapiro

Getty Images: Lucille Ball © Michael Ochs Archives, Norman Borlaug © Art Rickerby/Time & Life Pictures, Charlie Chaplin © American Stock, Albert Einstein © Ernst Haas, Mahatma Gandhi © Apic, Lou Gehrig © Transcendental Graphics,

Special thanks to Andy Miyares and the entire Miyares family, Special Olympics Florida, Officer Frank Shankwitz, the Make-A-Wish Foundation of Arizona, TeamHoyt.com, the family of Jim Hanson, Bernard Gotfryd, the legendary Robert Lerner, Joanne Siegel, Laura Siegel Larson, Norma Sue Hanson and everyone at Case Western Reserve University's Kelvin Smith Library, Bradley Ricca, Heifer International and the people at Heifer.org, Nick Raposo for sharing his dad's song, Alexis Soto and everyone at HaleHouse.org, and my friend Phyllis Segal.

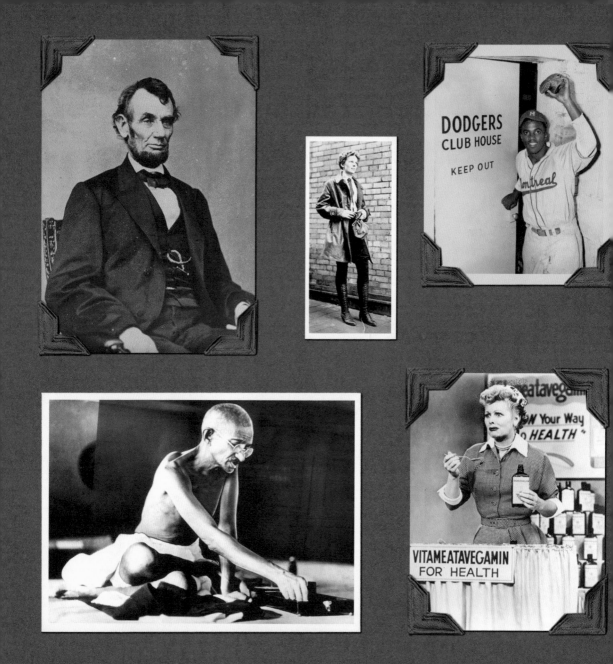